# UNDERSTANDING

# NEURO-LINGUISTIC PROGRAMMING

## Master The Art Of Influence And Communication For Effective Communication, Personal Development, Transformation, Success And More

## DR. KARSON BRYAN

## DISCLAIMER

This book's content is meant to be used solely for general informative purposes. Despite having taken every precaution to guarantee the content's accuracy, the author disclaims all duty and responsibility for any errors or omissions. It is recommended that readers exercise caution and, if needed, seek expert guidance. Any and all liability for losses, damages, or other outcomes arising from the use of the material included in this book is disclaimed by the author and publisher. All referenced product names and trademarks are the property of their respective owners and are merely cited for identification. Any likeness to real people or things is entirely accidental. Since it is a work of fiction, this book should not be used as a substitute for professional, legal, or medical advice. It is advised that readers seek advice on particular issues from qualified experts."

Please make sure that this disclaimer is modified to fit the particular requirements and subject matter of your book. Seeking advice from a legal expert is also a smart option if you have any questions or require a more thorough disclaimer for your specific book.

# TABLE OF CONTENTS


CHAPTER ONE ...................................................................8

NEURO-LINGUISTIC PROGRAMMING ........................................8

INTRODUCTION ...............................................................8

WHAT IS NEURO-LINGUISTIC PROGRAMMING? .....................8

THE EVOLUTION AND HISTORIES OF NLP THERAPY ...........9

THE FUNDAMENTALS OF NLP COUNSELING .....................9

CHAPTER TWO ...............................................................12

THE BASICS OF NLP TREATMENT.......................................12

THE NLP COMMUNICATION MODEL ...............................12

NLP PRESUPPOSITIONS ..............................................13

PERCEPTION CLARITY AND ADJUSTMENT .....................14

DEVELOPING A RAPPORT AND COMMUNICATING ...........15

CHAPTER THREE ...........................................................16

KNOWING THE TECHNIQUES OF NLP .................................16

THE NLP COMMUNICATION MODEL ...............................16

REPRESENTATIONAL SYSTEMS .....................................17

SUBMODALITIES AND THEIR SIGNIFICANCE.....................19

TECHNIQUES FOR ANCHORING .....................................21

CHAPTER FOUR .............................................................24

NLP THERAPY APPLICATIONS ...........................................24

NLP IN PERSONAL DEVELOPMENT .................................24

NLP IN COMMUNICATION AND INFLUENCE .....................24

NLP IN GOAL SETTING AND ACHIEVEMENT .....................25

NLP IN RELATIONSHIPS AND CONFLICT RESOLUTION.......26

NLP FOR OVERCOMING FEARS AND PHOBIAS ..................................26

NLP IN STRESS MANAGEMENT................................................27

NLP FOR HEALTH AND WELL-BEING............................................28

CHAPTER FIVE............................................................30

ADVANCED TOPICS IN NLP .................................................30

TIME-BASED TECHNIQUES IN NLP...........................................30

MODELING EXCELLENCE....................................................31

ADVANCED LINGUISTIC PATTERNS IN NLP ...................................32

NEURO-LINGUISTIC PROGRAMMIG IN LEADERSHIP AND BUSINESS..33

NLP AND EMOTIONAL INTELLIGENCE .......................................33

COMBINING NLP WITH OTHER THERAPEUTIC APPROACHES.............34

CHAPTER SIX.............................................................36

PRACTICAL AND ETHICAL ASPECTS TO CONSIDER ...........................36

IN NLP THERAPY, ETHICS AND RESPONSIBILITY ...........................36

TRAINING AND CERTIFICATION FOR NLP PRACTITIONERS.................37

LOCATING A COACH OR PRACTITIONER OF NLP ............................39

FREQUENTLY HELD MYTHS AND CRITICISMS OF NLP.......................40

PROSPECTIVE PATTERNS AND ADVANCEMENTS IN NLP....................42

# CHAPTER ONE

# NEURO-LINGUISTIC PROGRAMMING

## INTRODUCTION

### WHAT IS NEURO-LINGUISTIC PROGRAMMING?

A comprehensive approach to psychotherapy and personal growth, neuro-linguistic programming (NLP) therapy emphasizes the relationship between language, taught behavioral patterns, and brain processes. In essence, it is a framework for comprehending and enhancing people's thought processes, interpersonal interactions, and interactions with their environment. To assist individuals in reaching their objectives, enhancing their well-being, and overcoming obstacles, NLP therapy incorporates components of cognitive psychology, linguistics, and other therapeutic techniques.

# THE EVOLUTION AND HISTORIES OF NLP THERAPY

The origins of NLP therapy can be found in the 1970s, mainly in the research conducted by Richard Bandler and John Grinder. Together, linguist Grinder and mathematician Bandler studied and modeled the actions and speech patterns of prominent therapists like Fritz Perls and Milton H. Erickson. Their goal was to extract the key elements that contributed to these therapists' remarkable success in assisting clients in altering their attitudes and actions. The outcome of this cooperative endeavor was the development of NLP, a flexible and impactful methodology within the domains of psychology and therapy.

## THE FUNDAMENTALS OF NLP COUNSELING

NLP therapy is based on several fundamental ideas. Above all, NLP is predicated on the notion that individuals function according to their internal models of the world, which mold their attitudes and actions. This implies that the way we perceive and engage with reality is greatly influenced by our unique experiences and ideas. NLP therapy places a strong emphasis on the necessity of comprehending and altering these internal models to bring about good transformation and personal development.

The idea of sensory perception is another essential component of NLP therapy. It implies that people's five senses sight, hearing, touch, taste, and smell are the main ways in which they take in the environment. As this can result in changes in emotional responses and behaviors, NLP therapists frequently work with clients to identify and adjust sensory representations connected with particular experiences or concerns.

Since communication is the link that separates people from the outside world and one another, it is essential to NLP therapy. NLP therapists focus on improving communication skills to create stronger relationships and affect positive change. They also pay close attention to language patterns, both verbal and nonverbal. They assist clients in being more conscious of how their language choices affect their relationships and results.

Developing rapport and solid interpersonal relationships is a fundamental component of NLP therapy. To build rapport and a sense of trust, building rapport entails mirroring and imitating the nonverbal behaviors of others. This idea can be especially helpful in therapeutic contexts when reaching goals requires cooperation and trust.

Neuro-Linguistic Programming (NLP) Therapy is an interdisciplinary approach to psychotherapy and personal development that incorporates elements of communication, psychology, and linguistics. It was created in the 1970s and is centered on comprehending and changing the internal models of the world that influence people's views and actions.

# CHAPTER TWO

# THE BASICS OF NLP TREATMENT

The foundation of NLP (Neuro-Linguistic Programming) therapy is based on a set of ideas and precepts that improve both interpersonal growth and efficient communication. We will cover a wide range of fundamental ideas in this talk, including the NLP Model of Communication, NLP Presuppositions, Sensory Acuity and Calibration, and Rapport Building and Communication.

## THE NLP COMMUNICATION MODEL

NLP as a field is built upon a core idea known as the NLP Model of Communication. It implies that different sensory pathways are at work during communication, which is a dynamic activity involving the speaker and the listener. The gustatory, tactile, olfactory, visual, and auditory modalities are among these sensory channels.

According to NLP, people process information through their senses, and knowing how to access these channels is essential for efficient communication. NLP practitioners can modify their communication to be more persuasive and impactful, building rapport and connection with others, by identifying and leveraging these channels.

## NLP PRESUPPOSITIONS

The fundamental ideas or precepts that underpin the NLP methodology are known as presuppositions. They are designed to be guiding presumptions that can result in more fruitful and efficient outcomes rather than absolute truths. Typical NLP presuppositions include "People make the best choice they can at any given moment," which emphasizes the idea that people typically act in ways they believe will benefit them, and "The map is not the territory," which suggests that our perception of reality is not the same as reality itself. These underlying assumptions help NLP practitioners develop a more adaptable and compassionate perspective, which is beneficial in therapeutic contexts.

## PERCEPTION CLARITY AND ADJUSTMENT

In NLP, the terms "sensory acuity" and "calibration" refer to the capacity to detect minute sensory cues that individuals make when speaking. NLP therapists receive training in cultivating enhanced sensory awareness, which enables them to identify alterations in an individual's tone, physiology, and linguistic preferences. Practitioners can learn about a person's mental state, emotional reactions, and communication congruence by tuning in to these clues. This ability is essential for establishing rapport and successfully assisting people in making positive changes in their lives.

# DEVELOPING A RAPPORT AND COMMUNICATING

Establishing rapport and communicating effectively are crucial components of NLP therapy. The development of a strong and harmonious relationship between the therapist and the client is referred to as rapport. Establishing a feeling of familiarity and trust entails mirroring and imitating the client's non-verbal cues, such as body language, tone, and breathing patterns. The therapist can more easily enable therapeutic change and help the client achieve their intended results when a good rapport has been established. The foundation of NLP therapy is effective communication within a good rapport since it promotes improved comprehension and teamwork.

the NLP Model of Communication, which acknowledges the significance of sensory channels in successful communication, serves as the foundation for the Foundations of NLP Therapy.

# CHAPTER THREE

# KNOWING THE TECHNIQUES OF NLP

## THE NLP COMMUNICATION MODEL

The basic idea of the NLP (Neuro-Linguistic Programming) communication model is the basis for comprehending how people view and engage with their environment. This model's foundation is the notion that our experiences are filtered through our senses before being affected by our minds, which in turn causes a range of emotions and behaviors. Three essential elements make up the NLP communication model: input, processing, and output.

The sensory organs through which we perceive the outside world visual (sight), auditory (sound), kinesthetic (touch and body sensations), olfactory (smell), and gustatory (taste)are included in the "input" stage. These sensory inputs play a critical role in forming our experiences and are in charge of obtaining information about our surroundings.

The internal mental processes that take place after sensory information is acquired are included in the "processing" stage. Information can be filtered, generalized, and removed in this way depending on personal ideas, values, and prior experiences. These inner workings have a big influence on how we perceive and understand the world.

Our processed sensory data is transformed into actions, emotions, and behaviors at the "output" stage. At this moment, we respond to our surroundings and interact with people using the internal image of the world that we have created. Comprehending this model enables NLP practitioners to examine and perhaps alter the many phases of communication to improve results in both personal and professional settings.

## REPRESENTATIONAL SYSTEMS

In natural language psychology, representational systems are the sensory modalities people use to encode and interpret information. These modalities can be broadly divided into three systems: kinesthetic, aural, and visual. Every individual has a chosen representational system that shapes their understanding of and interactions with the outside world. Gaining an awareness of and comprehension of these systems helps enhance interpersonal relationships and communication.

The term "visual representational systems" describes how people interpret and represent their experiences mostly via the use of visual cues. Individuals who prefer to communicate visually may say things like "I see what you mean" and are more likely to employ vivid descriptions or mental images when communicating.

The core of auditory representational systems is the processing and communication of information through the use of auditory signals, including words, noises, and voice tone. People who use this approach more frequently may say things like

"That sounds good to me" and frequently communicate verbally and visually.

Emotions, physiological experiences, and physical sensations are all connected to kinesthetic representational systems. Individuals who have a kinesthetic preference concentrate on physical and emotional sensations in their communication, making them more perceptive to their feelings and likely to use statements like "I feel that's right."

NLP practitioners can improve the efficacy of communication by adapting their rapport-building and communication strategies to the preferred mode of the other person by having a thorough understanding of that person's representational system.

## SUBMODALITIES AND THEIR SIGNIFICANCE

Submodalities are subtle variations and characteristics that exist within every representational system and have the potential to profoundly impact our perception and processing of data. They can be used to influence little but significant shifts in our mental processes and emotional reactions; they function similarly to the building blocks of our mental representations. People can alter their internal sensations and reinterpret their views by adjusting submodalities.

Submodalities within the visual system, for instance, might include the color, location, brightness, and size of mental representations. A person can modify the emotional impact of a memory or mental image by adjusting these submodalities. Submodalities in the auditory system include tone, volume, distance, and speed. By adjusting these submodalities, we can change how we interpret language and our internal conversation.

# TECHNIQUES FOR ANCHORING

Anchoring is a basic NLP technique that can be used to instantly establish and activate particular emotional or resourceful states. It entails associating a specific emotional state with external stimuli, such as a touch, a speech, or a gesture (the anchor). The person can use the anchor to access their preferred emotional state at any moment as it gets associated with them over time through repetition and association.

Applying anchoring can help with a variety of issues, such as anxiety management, confidence boosting, and stress reduction. For instance, in a deeply relaxed state, one can touch their thumb and forefinger together to create an anchor for relaxation. They will eventually be able to instantly induce a relaxed state whenever necessary by repeating this touch.

Reframing and reimprinting are NLP procedures that are intended to alter how someone perceives and interprets past events or beliefs. Reframing entails changing the context and meaning of a certain incident or circumstance to present a more empowered angle. This has the potential to be a very effective tool for changing negative mental habits and feelings into positive ones.

Reimprinting, on the other hand, is the process of going back to and reprograming memories or experiences from the past that have negatively affected an individual's life. Through the use of NLP approaches, people can improve their emotional health and behavior by altering how they recall and react to these prior experiences.

The Meta-Model and the Milton Model are two NLP linguistic frameworks that discuss how language affects perception and communication. A precise and analytical tool, the Meta-Model seeks to identify and confront ambiguous, restrictive, or distorted language patterns. It makes communication easier to understand and more effective by highlighting the speaker's underlying ideas and mental processes.

Conversely, the Milton Model is a collection of purposefully ambiguous language patterns meant to elicit trance-like experiences and encourage suggestibility and open-mindedness. In therapy settings, these patterns are frequently employed to help clients delve deeper into the exploration of their innermost feelings and thoughts.

In NLP, "strategies" refers to the mental and sensory patterns that people employ to complete particular tasks or reach their goals. These techniques can be dissected into their constituent parts, including behavioral execution, decision-making, and sensory representation. Analyzing and comprehending someone's strategies helps NLP practitioners assist individuals in enhancing their performance in numerous areas by adjusting and optimizing these mental processes.

# CHAPTER FOUR

# NLP THERAPY APPLICATIONS

## NLP IN PERSONAL DEVELOPMENT

Neuro-Linguistic Programming (NLP) has garnered prominence for its applications in personal development. It offers individuals a toolkit to better understand their thoughts, emotions, and behaviors, allowing them to identify and overcome self-limiting beliefs and patterns. NLP techniques help in enhancing self-awareness and self-esteem, enabling people to gain a clearer sense of their identity and purpose in life. Through practices like anchoring and reframing, NLP empowers individuals to change their mental and emotional states, fostering personal growth and self-improvement.

## NLP IN COMMUNICATION AND INFLUENCE

Effective communication is a vital skill in both personal and professional contexts. NLP provides valuable tools for improving one's communication abilities and understanding the communication styles of others. Techniques like rapport-building, mirroring, and matching enable individuals to establish stronger connections with others. Additionally, NLP helps in mastering persuasive language patterns and non-verbal cues, making it easier to influence and persuade others positively, whether in sales, negotiation, or leadership.

## NLP IN GOAL SETTING AND ACHIEVEMENT

Setting and achieving goals is a fundamental aspect of personal and professional success. NLP offers a structured approach to goal setting and achievement by helping individuals clarify their goals, make them more specific and compelling, and overcome any mental barriers that may hinder progress. Visualizing success, using well-formed outcomes, and leveraging the power of neuro-linguistic techniques such as submodalities can significantly improve one's ability to set and reach ambitious objectives.

## NLP IN RELATIONSHIPS AND CONFLICT RESOLUTION

Healthy relationships are built on effective communication and understanding. NLP equips individuals with tools to improve their interpersonal skills, fostering better relationships with friends, family, and colleagues. It teaches techniques for empathetic listening, resolving conflicts, and understanding the perspectives of others. By enhancing emotional intelligence and facilitating rapport, NLP aids in building stronger, more harmonious relationships and resolving conflicts constructively.

## NLP FOR OVERCOMING FEARS AND PHOBIAS

Phobias and irrational fears can severely limit one's quality of life. NLP is known for its effective strategies to help individuals overcome such fears and phobias. Through techniques like the Fast Phobia Cure, NLP enables people to reframe and desensitize the negative emotions associated with their fears, allowing them to regain control and live more fulfilling lives. This can be applied to a wide range of fears, from public speaking to flying.

## NLP IN STRESS MANAGEMENT

Stress is a common modern-day challenge that can lead to various physical and mental health issues. NLP provides stress management techniques that help individuals better cope with stressors. These techniques may include relaxation and visualization exercises, anchoring positive emotional states, and reframing stressful situations. NLP assists in reprogramming the mind to respond more calmly and resourcefully to stressful circumstances, promoting overall well-being.

# NLP FOR HEALTH AND WELL-BEING

NLP can also play a role in enhancing health and well-being. It emphasizes the mind-body connection and how thoughts and emotions can impact physical health. Through techniques like timeline therapy, NLP can help individuals address past traumas and negative emotions that may be affecting their well-being. By improving mental and emotional states, NLP can contribute to better physical health outcomes and overall well-being.

NLP offers a diverse range of applications in personal development, communication, goal setting, relationships, fear and phobia management, stress reduction, and health and well-being. By utilizing the principles and techniques of NLP, individuals can transform their lives, fostering personal growth, success, and improved mental and physical health.

# CHAPTER FIVE

# ADVANCED TOPICS IN NLP

## TIME-BASED TECHNIQUES IN NLP

NLP's Time-Based Techniques are a potent collection of instruments and approaches that center on how humans experience and connect to time. These methods are used by NLP practitioners to assist people in managing their time perceptions more effectively, which helps them overcome obstacles and accomplish their objectives. A popular time-based method is the "TimeLine," which is a person's internalized concept of time. NLP practitioners can assist individuals in reframing their previous experiences, making plans for the future, and addressing procrastination, stress, and goal-setting concerns by using their TimeLine. The goal of time-based therapies like TimeLine therapy is to assist people in developing more resourceful and empowering connections with time.

# MODELING EXCELLENCE

A fundamental idea in NLP, modeling excellence is examining and imitating the attitudes, practices, and methods of people who achieve success in a given sector or aspect of life. NLP practitioners can assist others in reaching comparable accomplishment levels by comprehending the mental processes, linguistic patterns, and behavioral patterns of specialists. Usually, this approach entails dissecting the expert's actions into discernible and repeatable parts. After these elements are recognized, people who want to perform better can learn about them and incorporate them into their daily lives. NLP modeling excellence has applications in business, sports, the arts, and personal growth. It enables people to take advantage of the knowledge of professionals to improve their abilities and accomplishments.

# ADVANCED LINGUISTIC PATTERNS IN NLP

In NLP, advanced language patterns relate to the complex linguistic strategies employed to persuade and communicate more successfully. These patterns explore the subtleties of persuasion, rapport-building, and subconscious communication in addition to basic linguistic skills. These sophisticated language patterns are used by NLP practitioners to better comprehend and influence the ideas and actions of others. Communication strategies like hidden directives, presuppositions, and analogous marking are used to persuade people and get the results they want. These patterns apply to written communication as well as spoken language, which makes them useful tools in professions like marketing, sales, coaching, and therapy.

# NEURO-LINGUISTIC PROGRAMMIG IN LEADERSHIP AND BUSINESS

Neuro-Linguistic Programming has been applied extensively in both leadership and business domains. It offers methods and strategies for raising communication levels, strengthening leadership, and promoting organizational change. NLP enables leaders to develop more motivated and effective teams by helping them understand themselves and their teams better. Through the application of NLP techniques such as goal setting, rapport building, and modeling excellence, leaders may motivate and impact their teams to attain greater levels of productivity. Additionally, NLP can help with stress management, conflict resolution, and decision-making—all of which are crucial in leadership and corporate jobs.

## NLP AND EMOTIONAL INTELLIGENCE

A key component of both personal and professional success is emotional intelligence, which is the capacity to identify, comprehend, control, and affect one's own emotions as well as those of others. By offering resources to improve self-awareness, empathy, and successful communication, NLP supports emotional intelligence. By assisting people in identifying and controlling their emotions, NLP approaches enable people to react to difficult circumstances with greater expertise. Additionally, NLP helps with rapport-building and relationship enhancement, which are important aspects of emotional intelligence. NLP practitioners can gain a deeper understanding of nonverbal cues and emotional states by using techniques like sensory acuity and calibration, which can be extremely useful in both personal and professional settings.

## COMBINING NLP WITH OTHER THERAPEUTIC APPROACHES

To give patients seeking personal development and healing a more thorough and individualized course of care, NLP is frequently combined with other therapeutic approaches. NLP can improve therapy whether it is used in conjunction with psychoanalysis, counseling, or cognitive-behavioral therapy. It provides special tools for quick change and aids in trauma healing, phobia conquering, and negative belief reframing. NLP can offer a comprehensive and client-centered therapeutic experience when combined with other techniques, addressing both conscious and unconscious parts of a person's mind. A more flexible and successful therapeutic strategy that can accommodate the needs and preferences of a wide range of clients is made possible by this combination.

# CHAPTER SIX

# PRACTICAL AND ETHICAL ASPECTS TO CONSIDER

## IN NLP THERAPY, ETHICS AND RESPONSIBILITY

In the field of NLP (Neuro-Linguistic Programming) therapy, client safety and well-being are greatly dependent on ethical issues. NLP therapists and practitioners are held to the highest standards of responsibility and professionalism and are required to abide by a rigid code of ethics. The informed consent principle is one of the fundamental ethical tenets of NLP therapy. Clients must be completely aware of the objectives, methods, and nature of NLP therapy. Additionally, they ought to be free to decide whether or not to take part.

Confidentiality is another essential component of ethical NLP therapeutic practice. NLP practitioners are required to maintain the privacy of all client information, including private conversations and personal details. In many nations, protecting client privacy is not only legally required but also morally right. For practitioners, breaching client confidentiality can have dire repercussions.

NLP therapists also need to understand the power dynamics in the therapeutic alliance. They must make sure they don't abuse their power over customers. They ought to refrain from using deceptive methods and put the client's welfare ahead of their interests. To avoid any possible exploitation or injury, professional boundaries must be upheld.

## TRAINING AND CERTIFICATION FOR NLP PRACTITIONERS

To guarantee the efficacy and moral use of NLP therapy, NLP practitioners must complete training and certification requirements. Since NLP is not a regulated industry, there are many different NLP certification organizations and training programs available. People who are interested in NLP therapy should make sure that the practitioners they hire have received credible training.

A variety of subjects are covered in reputable NLP training programs, such as communication skills, ethics, NLP techniques, and the real-world applications of NLP in therapeutic settings. To obtain certification as a certified NLP practitioner, one must typically finish a training course and exhibit mastery of the fundamental NLP principles and procedures.

When selecting NLP practitioners who make expert claims without the necessary education and certification, clients should exercise caution. Asking a practitioner about their training history and the certification organization they belong to is a good idea. Clients can use this information to make well-informed decisions regarding the level of care they can anticipate.

# LOCATING A COACH OR PRACTITIONER OF NLP

Selecting the appropriate NLP coach or practitioner is an essential first step for anyone considering NLP therapy. The procedure entails thorough investigation and deliberation to guarantee that the practitioner is a suitable match for the client's requirements. The following procedures can assist in locating a certified NLP practitioner:

1. Research: Look up NLP practitioners online or in your community first. Check for their credentials, licenses, and areas of expertise.

2. Suggestions: Ask friends, relatives, or other reliable people who have had good experiences with NLP practitioners for suggestions. Personal recommendations have value.

3. Consultation: Get in touch with prospective teachers to arrange a consultation or first meeting. This enables you to evaluate their

methodology, mode of communication, and level of comfort in collaborating.

4. Credentials: Check the practitioner's qualifications, such as their certification in NLP and any applicable licenses or memberships in associations for professionals.

5. Ethics: Find out how they handle customer confidentiality and well-being, as well as their ethical standards. Make sure they share your expectations and values.

6. Experience: Take into account the practitioner's years of experience as well as their history of assisting clients in realizing their objectives.

7. Cost: Talk about the session fees as well as any possible insurance or payment plans.

## FREQUENTLY HELD MYTHS AND CRITICISMS OF NLP

Like many therapeutic modalities, NLP is not without its detractors and myths. To obtain a more precise comprehension of NLP therapy, it is vital to tackle them.

One prevalent misunderstanding is that mind control is a function of NLP. Rather than focusing on managing or influencing people, NLP aims to understand and enhance communication and cognitive patterns. Instead of exercising control over their clients, ethical NLP practitioners empower them with their expertise.

Many times, detractors claim that NLP is not supported by actual science. Even while NLP has had difficulty living up to the demanding criteria of empirical study, it has nevertheless assisted a great number of people in achieving good change and personal development. The benefits that many clients have experienced in the real world are not diminished by the lack of scientific consensus.

NLP is criticized for being unduly basic and for failing to take into consideration the complexities of psychology and human behavior. Although NLP offers useful tools for transformation, it cannot fully replace other therapeutic modalities. To provide a more comprehensive therapeutic experience, many practitioners combine NLP with additional techniques.

## PROSPECTIVE PATTERNS AND ADVANCEMENTS IN NLP THERAPY

The field of NLP therapy is always developing due to new developments in research, technology, and client needs. The future of NLP therapy is being shaped by several trends and advancements.

1. internet and Remote Therapy: NLP and other internet therapies gained popularity during the COVID-19 pandemic. In addition to giving clients access to NLP therapy from the comforts of their homes, remote sessions give practitioners the chance to address a worldwide clientele.

2. Integrative Approaches: To provide clients with more all-encompassing answers, NLP practitioners

are progressively combining aspects from other therapeutic methods, such as mindfulness and cognitive-behavioral therapy (CBT).

3. Personalized NLP: In the future, NLP treatments might be customized to each client's unique requirements and preferences using AI and data analytics, which would increase the efficacy of therapy.

4. Ethical rules: To guarantee responsible and professional activity among NLP practitioners, it is expected that as the field develops, more standardized ethical rules and regulatory bodies will be established.

5. Research and Evidence: Continued efforts to close the knowledge gap between NLP and empirical research may result in a greater comprehension of the advantages and disadvantages of NLP methods.

NLP therapy is a dynamic area with changing training standards, ethical obligations, and criticisms and misconceptions to take into account. When selecting a practitioner, clients seeking NLP therapy should be well-informed and cautious. To better assist clients, NLP will probably continue to evolve and incorporate new technology and research findings as the therapeutic landscape changes.